Isbn 13: 978-18464-6199-6
Isbn 10: 1-8464-6199-5

Published by Ladybird Books Ltd.
A Penguin Company
Penguin Books Ltd, 80 Strand, London, WC2R ORL, UK
Penguin Books, Australia Ltd, Camberwell, Victoria, Australia
Penguin Group (NZ), 67 Apollo Drive, Mairangi Bay,
Auckland, New Zealand

2 4 6 8 10 9 7 5 3 1

LADYBIRD and the device of a ladybird are trademarks of Ladybird Books Ltd.

Printed in Italy

HAPPY FEET

In the coldest place on Earth - Antarctica -
the air was full of song. It was mating season
for the Emperor penguins. Each penguin
hoped to attract a soul-mate by serenading
them with their special personal melody
- their Heartsong.

Two voices stood out from the rest - those of the lovely Norma Jean and the tall, handsome Memphis. As their Heartsongs blended, their singing became love. And before long, their love became an egg.

Winter arrived, and Norma Jean had to go and hunt for fish in the waters far away with the other females, leaving Memphis to care for their precious egg.

As the male penguins huddled together to protect their eggs from the bitter weather, Noah the Elder led the ritual chanting, urging the Great Guin to keep them safe.

'Make a Huddle.'

'Warm thy egg.'

'Make a Huddle.'

'Share the cold.'

But Memphis, distracted by thoughts of Norma Jean, did the unthinkable. He dropped his egg - a terrible thing for a penguin to do.

At last, the sun returned - and with it, the mother penguins.

Memphis was anxious as he waited to be reunited with Norma Jean. Their egg had finally hatched, but long after all the others. And their hatchling son - Mumble - had the most unusual tap-happy feet.

'I wouldn't do that around folks, son,' said Memphis quietly, as Mumble hippity-hopped around. 'It ain't penguin.'

But Norma Jean, home at last, didn't care.

'Oh, Memphis,' she cried as she cuddled her son, 'he's gorgeous!'

At Penguin Elementary, the hatchlings were soon learning their most important lesson.

'Does anyone know what it is?' asked Miss Viola.

'It's our Heartsongs, Miss,' answered Gloria, brightest of the girl chicks. 'It's the voice you hear inside. The voice of who you truly are.'

But when Mumble tried to share his Heartsong, his classmates laughed. His singing voice was completely tuneless. Instead of melody, Mumble's heart swelled with rhythm.

He was an oddity - a penguin without a Heartsong.

Time passed quickly. Before long, the young penguins had lost their infant fluff and were ready to graduate. All except Mumble. Still fluffy, he was once again the odd one out.

And things got worse. When Gloria sang at the graduation party, Mumble, love-struck, couldn't help joining in. The other penguins didn't appreciate his tuneless screeching.

'Keep it down, weirdo!'

'What's wrong with you?!'

Mumble withdrew sadly to a nearby ice floe, and slipped into a lonely sleep.

The next morning, Mumble woke suddenly when something jolted the ice floe from beneath. He had floated a long way. The rocky shore nearby, homeland of the small-but-spirited Adelie penguins, was unfamiliar.

A second, larger jolt tipped Mumble into the icy water - he was being attacked by a hungry Leopard Seal!

Terrified, Mumble swam for his life, just managing to escape the seal's fearsome jaws. He burst from the water to the safety of land, with a stylish, acrobatic leap.

'Whoaaaaaa! Goal!'

'You da bomb, bro!'

'I give you a 10!'

Five little Adelie penguins with big attitudes cheered Mumble's graceful landing. When Mumble showed them some of his dance moves, they were even more impressed.

'Oh yeah! - I like it, Tall Boy!'

Ramon, leader of the 'Amigos', invited Mumble to return to their colony with them. Mumble soon discovered that life in Adelie Land was one long Mambo dance party!

And the Adelies liked Mumble because he was different.

Mumble had great fun with his new friends
- particularly when they accidentally took a
wild slide ride together, over an ice-cliff,
down into the sea below.

Underwater, the penguins discovered
a twisted, lifeless creature. It was unlike
anything they had ever seen before.

Mumble had once met a skua bird who
claimed he had been abducted by 'Aliens'.
He wondered if this mysterious monster
had something to do with the same Alien
beings.

'You want answers?' asked Ramon. 'You
go see Lovelace!'

Lovelace was a Rockhopper penguin who lived nearby. He had convinced the Adelie penguins that the strange set of rings around his neck were a sign of his connection with 'Mystic Beings'. The Adelies came to him with questions, paying for his advice with pebbles.

Mumble queued at Lovelace's impressive pebble pile. At last, it was his turn.

'Were you abducted by Aliens?' he asked.

'What kind of question is that?!' exclaimed Lovelace.

And refusing to answer, he withdrew.

As Mumble walked away, disappointed, Ramon asked him about Emperor Land.

'Hey, Stretch - you got any stones where you come from?'

For the Adelies, the biggest pebble pile meant the best chance of attracting a mate.

'We don't collect stones,' replied Mumble. He explained about Heartsongs, and about how his own inability to sing meant he had no hope of winning his sweetheart, Gloria.

But Ramon wasn't so sure.

'Don't worry,' he said. 'We can fix it . . .'

Back in Emperor Land, the young penguins were in full song. No other voice compared to that of Gloria.

As she sang her beautiful Heartsong, male admirers jostled around her, trying to woo her with their songs.

Suddenly, another soaring voice drew everyone's attention. Mumble had returned to Emperor Land and was singing as never before. But Gloria quickly discovered the truth - Ramon was hiding behind Mumble's back, singing on his behalf.

'Mumble - how could you?' said Gloria, disappointed. Mumble was desperate to make things right.

'Gloria . . . sing to this,' he implored, tapping out a catchy rhythm with his feet.

And as Mumble's feet tippety-tapped, Gloria, despite herself, was captivated. Soon she was singing her heart out!

Together her singing and his dancing become one and the power of their Heartsong grew and grew.

Soon, other young penguins, following Mumble's lead, began to sing and dance to Gloria's funky Heartsong. Before long, 'happy feet' had really taken hold!

'STOP THIS UNRULY NONSENSE!'

Noah the Elder brought the dance party to an abrupt end.

The colony was suffering a famine. The Elders were convinced it was Mumble's un-Emperor-like behaviour - his 'freakiness with the feet' - that had caused the fish shortage, by offending the Great Guin.

When Memphis confessed his dreadful secret - that he had dropped Mumble as an egg - the Elders' suspicions only worsened.

'You, Mumble Happy Feet, must go!' shrieked Noah, banishing Mumble from the colony.

Mumble knew his only hope for returning home was to discover the real cause of the fish shortage. He was sure the Aliens would know, and led the Amigos back to Lovelace's pebble pile, determined to find out more about his 'Mystic Beings'.

They found Lovelace in big trouble. The rings around his neck were making it difficult for him to breathe. Unable to speak, he explained to them through mime how he had really acquired the rings - while swimming in far-off waters, along the Forbidden Shore.

Convinced it was the only way to find help for Lovelace - and find out what had happened to the fish - Mumble set out with his friends for the Forbidden Shore.

The penguins passed through the Land of the Elephant Seals, where two enormous seals warned them that the terrible beings who inhabited their destination:

'Annihilate every livin' thing in their path!'

But Mumble led his friends on, across the wilds of the Great Glacier and Blizzard Country, until, exhausted, they slept.

When Mumble and the Amigos awoke, Lovelace had vanished. They followed his footsteps to an eerie, Alien place, full of terrifying-looking contraptions - a deserted whaling station.

'The Forbidden Shore!' said Mumble, awestruck.

They found Lovelace, barely breathing, by the water's edge. He was pointing at a collection of floating junk, which included several rings like his own collar.

'Hang in there, Lovelace,' said Mumble, convinced the Aliens must be nearby. 'I know they're here somewhere!'

Suddenly, two enormous killer whales leapt from the water, smashing through the ice on which the penguins were standing.

Mumble and Lovelace couldn't escape the hungry whales. But as the whales had fun tossing them back and forth, Lovelace was freed at last from his choking collar. He quickly used his regained voice to give the whales a piece of his mind.

'You flaccid-finned overblown baitfish!' he yelled. 'Hightail it back to your mommas!'

To the penguins' astonishment, the

ferocious whales did turn and swim away.
But the real reason quickly became clear,
as a colossal black shape loomed out of the
ghostly fog.

'Not in my wildest dreams . . .'
murmured Mumble.

From the highest point on the glacier,
Mumble watched the Alien vessel join a fleet
of others out at sea. Mumble had found the
Aliens at last. He said a hasty farewell to his
bewildered friends, dived fearlessly into the
water, and swam after it.

Close up, Mumble saw the vessel drag the ocean with huge nets, and he finally understood the reason for the fish shortage.

'Hey - you're taking our fish! Wait!'

But the fishermen ignored him. As the vessels headed for the open sea, Mumble gave chase.

For days he swam, until exhaustion finally overcame him.

When he awoke, he found himself in penguin heaven. Mumble had been put in a zoo, having been found, half-dead, washed up on a polluted beach.

Every day, groups of Aliens came to stare at him.

'Why are you taking our fish?' Mumble demanded. 'We can't survive without them!'

But Mumble couldn't make the Aliens understand his vital message. All hope lost, he slipped steadily into the same zombie-like state as the other captive penguins.

Then, one day, a little Alien visited the zoo. When she tapped on the glass, Mumble instinctively echoed her taps with his feet. Soon, his tap-dancing had drawn a delighted crowd.

At last he had found a way to communicate with the Aliens - dance!

Soon after, Mumble was hippity-hopping across the pack ice towards his home. Scientists had returned him to Antarctica, electronically tagged, so they could find out exactly where this remarkable dancing penguin had come from.

Mumble was overjoyed to find his sweetheart Gloria still waiting for him. But not everyone in Emperor Land was pleased to see him.

'SO! YOU DARE COME BACK!' bellowed Noah.

And when Mumble revealed his discovery - that Aliens had been taking their fish - the

Elders were unconvinced.

Then, suddenly, a helicopter roared across the sky. The terrified Elders could doubt the Aliens' existence no longer. As their only chance to save themselves, Mumble led the colony in a spectacular tap-dancing display.

Amid the thousands of dancing penguins, Mumble was reunited with his mother, Norma Jean, and his friends, the Amigos.

And after a little persuasion, even Mumble's father Memphis, reconciled to his son's unusual gift at last, joined in with the dancing.

The helicopter landed and a group of Aliens climbed out.

The penguins' dance display - led by Mumble and Gloria - grew more and more breathtaking.

Then, as the Aliens clapped out rhythms, the vast crowd of penguins tap-danced them back to them - the two species were communicating!

'It's working!' Mumble yelled. 'Keep dancing!'

It was clear that this marvel of nature had to

be preserved at all costs. Fishing in Antarctic waters was immediately banned, to ensure the survival of these remarkable beings.

So, thanks to Mumble Happy Feet, a brave and gifted young penguin who had undertaken a long and dangerous journey to finally belong, the penguins of Antarctica once again had plenty to eat - something they could really make a song and dance about!